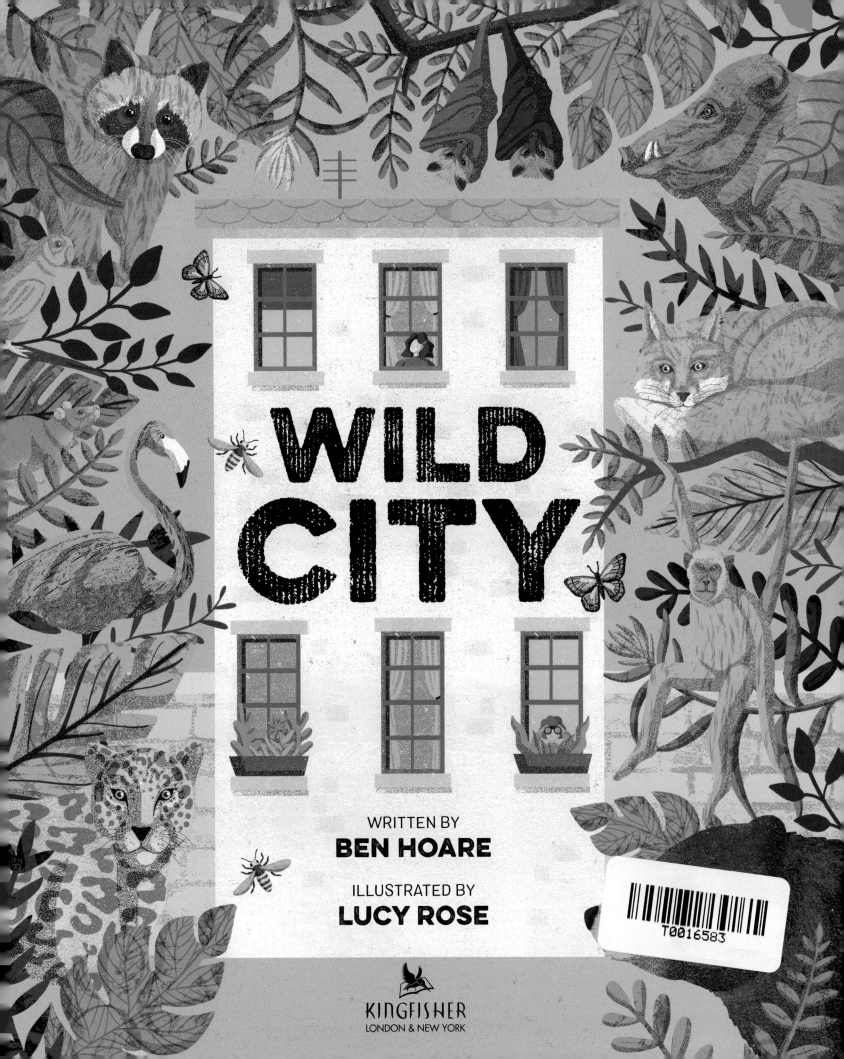

WILD CITY

WRITTEN BY
BEN HOARE

ILLUSTRATED BY
LUCY ROSE

KINGFISHER
LONDON & NEW YORK

For Louise and our two beautiful girls—B. H.

For Hilary and Mick—L. R.

For Liam—L. H.

KINGFISHER
LONDON & NEW YORK

Text copyright © Macmillan Publishers International Ltd 2020, 2022
Illustrations copyright © Lucy Rose 2020, 2022
First published 2020 in the United Stated by Kingfisher
This edition published in 2022 in the United Stated by Kingfisher
120 Broadway, New York, NY 10271
Kingfisher is an imprint of Macmillan Chilldren's Books, London

ISBN 978-0-7534-7633-8 (HC)
978-0-7534-7764-9 (PB)

Distributed in the U.S. and Canda by Macmillan,
120 Broadway, New York, NY 10271

Library of Congress Cataloging-in-Publication data has been applied for.

Concept and design: Laura Hall
Senior editor: Lizzie Davey

Kingfisher Books are available for special promotions and premiums.
For details contact:
Special Markets Department, Macmillan,
120 Broadway, New York, NY 10271

For more information please visit:
www.kingfisherbooks.com

Printed in China
2 4 6 8 9 7 5 3 1
1TR/0622/UG/WKT/140WF

EU representative: 1st Floor, The Liffey Trust Centre,
117-126 Sheriff Street Upper, Dublin 1 D01 YC43

WILD CITY

WRITTEN BY

BEN HOARE

ILLUSTRATED BY

LUCY ROSE

More and more of us live in cities and towns. Already, over half of all the world's people is urban. But in the urban jungle, you're never far from wildlife. Whether your home is a vast city or a small one, a town or a suburb, it is sure to have exciting wildlife too.

We see some of these wild animals all the time—pigeons and insects such as ants, for example. Other creatures are so good at hiding or moving quietly around the city, we don't even know they are there. But they're there, all right. From parrots to penguins, bats to bears, and spiders to snakes, these animals are perfectly at home on our doorstep.

Are you surprised that an animal as big as a bear would want to live in a city? Think about it, though. The words "city" and "country" mean nothing to animals. They don't see any difference. Animals just want a safe place to live, where they can find food and shelter and raise a family. Cities can give them all these things.

Of course, many of the animals and plants living in cities are found in wild areas. Every city has quiet corners like these. They include urban woods and parks, rivers, and canals. However, size doesn't matter. A backyard or balcony, flowerbed or puddle is big enough to be a wildlife habitat.

This book introduces some of the amazing wildlife that shares our cities. You will also meet a few wildlife heroes from around the world—ordinary people doing extraordinary things to make our wild neighbors feel welcome.

Ben Hoare

VANCOUVER
8-9

STOCKHOLM
32-33

LONDON
24-25

BERLIN
28-29

SEVILLE
36-37

ASPEN
14-15

NEW YORK
10-11

MEXICO CITY
18-19

RIO de JANEIRO
20-21

CAPE TOWN
44-45

CONTENTS

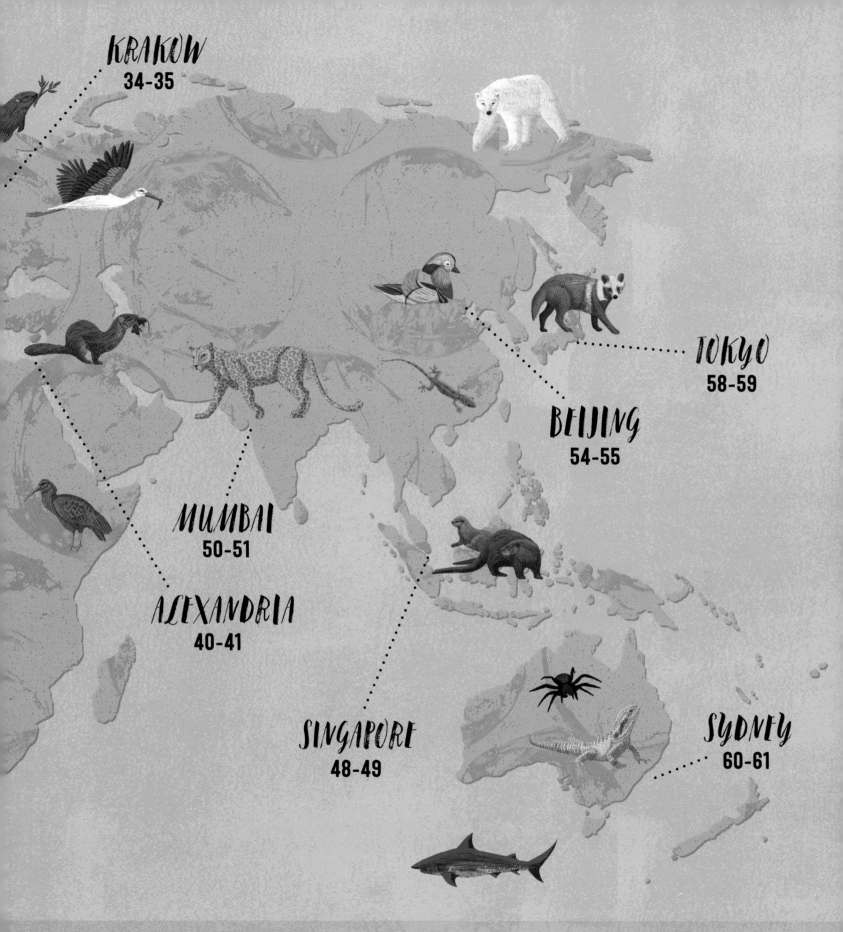

KRAKOW
34-35

TOKYO
58-59

BEIJING
54-55

MUMBAI
50-51

ALEXANDRIA
40-41

SINGAPORE
48-49

SYDNEY
60-61

VANCOUVER

Between forested mountains and the deep blue sea lies Vancouver. This port has a spectacular location on the west coast of Canada, facing the Pacific Ocean. Skyscrapers line the shore, and ships of all kinds share the cold Pacific waters with a host of sea creatures, from glittering schools of fish to mighty whales.

HUMPBACK WHALE

These enormous mammals show up in the summer. Scientists recognize the same humpback whales returning every year. They come to feed on fish. In the winter they swim thousands of miles south to have young.

*Male humpback whales sing **strange** and **beautiful** songs.*

ORCA

Giant triangular fins in the bay mean orcas are around! Several of their family groups, called "pods," live along the Vancouver coast. Summer is when orcas come closest to the city—they work together to hunt salmon.

CHINOOK SALMON

Salmon are powerful, muscular fish. They hatch in streams and then head out to the Pacific Ocean to feed and grow. They then swim back upstream to where their life began, passing Vancouver as they go.

The **North Shore** mountain range overlooks Vancouver. It is home to **eagles** and **bears.**

GREAT BLUE HERON

Herons patrol the shoreline and wade into the shallows to catch fish. They nest in the trees of Stanley Park, making one of the largest heron colonies of any North American city.

Each **orca** has its own black and white **pattern.**

HARBOR SEAL

Along rocky shores, seals are a common sight. They eat fish and squid, but they need to watch out for hungry orcas or they may end up on the menu.

RED-TAILED HAWK

These birds of prey often soar over the park. Tall buildings are just like cliffs to them, so make perfect nest sites. The story of a popular "red-tail" named Pale Male has featured in books and a documentary.

PEREGRINE

If New Yorkers look up, they might see the fastest bird on Earth flash past. The peregrine falcon dives from on high to catch pigeons and other birds in midair. It nests on many famous landmarks, including the Empire State Building and Brooklyn Bridge.

Central Park covers 840 acres (340 ha) of America's **biggest city.**

WOOD DUCK

As spectacular as any parrot, the male wood duck is one that's hard to miss. Like the local mallards, it soon becomes tame when people throw it handfuls of grain.

Terrapins snooze through the winter, safe in mud at the bottom of the pond.

EASTERN CHIPMUNK

Scampering around the bushes and paths are little striped squirrels. These are chipmunks, and they're hunting nuts. Often they stuff their cheeks full and then run off to bury the nuts for snacking on later.

RED-EARED TERRAPIN

Turtle Pond is home to—you guessed it—five or six species of turtles. Many are pets set free by their owners. In the summer you can spot terrapins sunbathing on rocks at the water's edge.

NEW YORK

New York stars in many songs and movies, and people call it the "Big Apple" or "the city that never sleeps." Right in the very heart of it is Central Park. This wild area has high-rise buildings on all sides but includes several ponds and 18,000 trees. It's a peaceful sanctuary for both wildlife and people.

As it dives, a **peregrine** can hit speeds of up to **186 mph (300 kph)**.

WHITE-FOOTED MOUSE

Crumbs dropped by people as they stroll through the park are guzzled by white-footed mice. Compared with country mice, these city mice have a very different diet and life, so their bodies are slowly changing. One day, they might become a new species.

MANHATTANT

Scientists on their lunch break discovered a new ant. It lives in New York and nowhere else on Earth. Its nickname is the 'ManhattAnt,' after Manhattan, the main island on which New York is built.

Each year the **ants** of one New York street **carry away food** weighing the same as **60,000 hot dogs.**

CITY BIRDS

There is so much more to the bird life of our cities than pigeons. From parrots to turkeys and owls, a surprising variety of species can be found right under our noses. Birds have the advantage that they are able to fly, which makes it easy for them to move into built-up areas. Some visit only at certain times of the year, or just for the night, while others live in our streets, parks, and backyards all year round.

GREAT TIT

All that traffic noise means birds struggle to be heard. But the great tits that live in European cities have started to sing louder than their country cousins. Their voices are also higher pitched to help their song soar above the background din.

KINGFISHER

As long as there are small fish to be found, the kingfisher can live in the heart of a city, such as London. If there are no waterside trees to perch on, then metal railings or a floating shopping cart will do.

LONG-EARED OWL

Each winter 700 of these owls roost together in Kikinda, a Serbian city in southeastern Europe. As they line up in the branches, they look like fluffy Christmas-tree ornaments! It is a rare treat to see so many owls at once.

STARLING

Those aren't clouds of black smoke, but huge flocks of starlings that whirl and swirl in the sky. Winter sunset gatherings are called murmurations. Up to a million starlings from far and wide roost in Rome's avenues of plane trees. They perform an aerial spectacular as beautiful as any ballet before they settle down for the night.

BRUSH TURKEY

Lawns and gardens on Australia's east coast are visited by a huge black "chicken" with a bare red head. The brush turkey's rain-forest habitat is disappearing, so it is moving into backyards. It builds a mighty mound of soil and dead leaves, then buries its eggs in this warm and sweaty heap to incubate them.

WATTLED IBIS

With its long, curved bill, there is no mistaking this crow-size bird. The wattled ibis is a common sight on lawns in Addis Ababa, the capital of Ethiopia. It pokes the grass to feel for earthworms and beetle larvae hidden in the soil.

BLUE-AND-GOLD MACAW

People in Campo Grande, Brazil, have gotten used to hearing loud squawks overhead. The city's palm trees have been taken over by colorful macaws, which use them to nest. So popular are the parrots that they are now the symbol of the city. Macaws Square is named after them, and it's against the law to cut down any nesting tree.

ASPEN

High in the Rocky Mountains is Aspen, with snowy peaks on all sides. Many people used to work in silver mines here, but today this Colorado town is a famous ski resort. Wildlife flocks here from the nearby pine forests. It's not unusual to see bears wander into the city.

AMERICAN RED SQUIRREL

This busy animal is nuts about nuts. And pine cones! By expertly nibbling a spiky cone, it can reach the seeds inside. A squirrel easily gets through 100 cones a day. If you hear a chatter or a chirp, a bark or a growl, there's probably a squirrel around.

If a **red squirrel** spots a **hawk**, it sounds the alarm with a loud **Seet!** For danger on the ground, it **barks** instead.

NORTHERN FLICKER

This spotted woodpecker is not like the others. No hammering on tree trunks— it prefers to feed on the ground. Look for it hopping across lawns to lick up tasty ants.

Ant-eating **flickers** have one of the **longest**, stickiest **tongues** of any bird.

AMERICAN ROBIN

When Europeans arrived in North America 400 years ago, they saw a bird that reminded them of home. Because it had a red breast, they called it the American robin. Sometimes this robin nests in unusual places, such as streetlights and signs.

MAIN ST

Aspen is named after a beautiful kind of **tree**, whose leaves **dance** and **whisper** in the wind.

BLACK BEAR

Imagine if bears went through your garbage cans! In Aspen, that really happens. Hungry black bears leave the mountain forests to hunt for leftovers and scraps. Usually they visit in the fall when they need to fatten up for their long winter sleep.

COYOTE

In Aspen, coyotes are top dog. They look like small wolves—and howl a bit like them too. Come late afternoon or evening, the coyotes slink through the city. They're looking for rats, mice . . . and the occasional unlucky cat.

Trying to scare away **300-pound (135 kg)** adult **bears** is not a good idea. Better to leave them alone!

HUNTERS IN THE CITY

From big cats to sharks, the wildlife in our cities includes some very exciting predators. A predator is any animal that kills another animal for food. These species have found that cities can be excellent hunting grounds. Many predators travel long distances to find prey. They quietly stalk, crawl, slide, or swim around urban areas to track down their next meal.

MOUNTAIN LION

The vast city of Los Angeles, California, is famous for its movie and TV industry. But L.A. has wildlife stars as well as movie stars. North America's biggest cat is the mountain lion, or cougar. It prowls the hills around L.A. in search of deer and other prey. One cat, which scientists call P22, has been photographed in front of the "Hollywood" sign.

CALIFORNIA SEA LION

Sea lions are fast and graceful as they chase fish in the water. They also spend a lot of time on land, resting together. Groups of sea lions bellyflop onto special floating platforms in San Francisco's busy harbor. Here in the bay, they are safe from their worst enemies—orcas.

SLOWWORM

It's not a huge worm, or a small snake. What is it? A legless lizard! The slowworm slithers over the soil to hunt insects. Like all reptiles, it has cold blood, so it loves sunbathing to warm up. In Great Britain it often lives on waste ground, where a rusty old piece of sun-heated metal makes a nice warming platform.

BLACK MAMBA

The deadliest snake in Africa, the black mamba grows over 6.5 feet (2 m) long and moves faster than you can sprint. On the hunt for rats, it explores backyards in the suburbs of some South African cities. Just a couple of drops of its powerful venom could kill a human.

YELLOW SCORPION

Scorpions are moving into Brazil's concrete jungles. Why? They are mainly after cockroaches, a beetle-like insect, which they kill with a quick flick of their stretchy stinger. If these dangerous creatures enter houses, there's a simple way to find them. Shine a UV (ultraviolet) light on scorpions, and they glow bright blue!

BULL SHARK

Bull sharks are unusual—they can survive in fresh water as well as in the sea. The river in Brisbane, Australia, acts like a shark nursery. Young bull sharks up to 5 feet (1.5 m) long have been spotted in the center of the city.

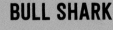

MEXICO CITY

The first canals were dug by the **Aztecs**, who ruled a mighty empire **600 years ago**.

Mexico City is gigantic and keeps growing, but to its south there is a maze of canals and lakes. Wildlife flocks to this peaceful place, especially birds. It is also the last home of the axolotl (ak–suh–lot–uhl), one of the weirdest animals on Earth. You can still find curious creatures even in a megacity like this one.

GREAT-TAILED GRACKLE

Anywhere you go in Mexico City, you will meet grackles. These noisy birds look black at first, but up close their feathers shimmer with purple and green. Grackles are sociable— they are always found in flocks.

Mexicans know this **watery wonderland** by its Spanish name: **Xochimilco (Soch–i–milko)**.

MEXICAN GARTER SNAKE

Snakes can be excellent swimmers. This slim, striped example glides through the water, moving its body in beautiful "S" shapes. Sometimes it floats with only its head peeping out. It hunts fish and frogs.

BLACK-CROWNED NIGHT HERON

Taking a trip on a boat called a gondola is a great way to spot wildlife. In waterside trees you might see small herons with long head feathers and red eyes. These are night herons. They sleep during the day and become active after sunset.

*An injured **axolotl** can grow a new **tail, eyes,** and **legs**—and even **repair** its **brain** and **heart**.*

AXOLOTL

This bizarre beast hides among waterweeds and mud at the water's bottom, where it catches worms. It is an amphibian, like frogs and toads. However, unlike them, it never grows up. An axolotl spends its whole life as a larva, similar to a big, fat tadpole.

BLUE-WINGED TEAL

These urban wetlands attract many wild ducks, including some from far away. Thousands of teal fly here from the U.S. and Canada for the winter, then return north in the spring.

BLUE MORPHO

These huge and beautiful butterflies look like glittering pieces of bright blue sky. They flap steadily around parks, as if in slow motion. The underside of their wings is camouflaged, so when they close their wings, they seem to disappear.

RED-NECKED TANAGER

Tanagers are small forest birds with jewel-like feathers that sparkle in the sun. Many different kinds flit about in Rio's parks. One is the red-necked tanager, which can't resist fresh fruit. People tie bananas to branches for it to eat.

In the **undergrowth** lives the curious **agouti**—a cross between a **rat** and a **rabbit**.

CHANNEL-BILLED TOUCAN

Froggy croaks coming from a treetop will lead you to this impressive bird. Its giant bill is much lighter than it looks, because it's hollow with thin sides. The toucan uses it to pick juicy fruit from the treetops.

RIO de JANEIRO

A huge statue of **Jesus Christ** looks out over the city, with **lush forest** all around it.

Rio has mountains and forest on one side, and sandy beaches and Atlantic surf on the other. It is the second-largest city in Brazil, but very important for wildlife. As more of the country's forests are cut down, the green areas left in Rio provide a safe place for many animals and plants. When you walk through its lush parks, the colorful birds and monkeys make you feel like you're in a rain forest.

People flock to **Rio's parks** to escape the **heat** of the city.

COMMON MARMOSET

With their white ear tufts, these mini monkeys look adorable. They are called "mico" in Portuguese, the language spoken in Brazil. A marmoset mother usually has twins. Each baby weighs about as much as a tennis ball, and the whole family helps feed them.

BLACK-AND-WHITE TEGU

Flowerbeds and lawns are ruled by big lizards up to 3 feet (1 m) long. Though they can appear sleepy, they're always alert, with a pink tongue that flicks in and out to taste the air. They sniff out fruit dropped by messy monkeys or toucans.

Marmosets squeak constantly to **stay in touch.**

21

CITY MAMMALS

All around the world, wild mammals have adapted to a new life in cities. Many of them, such as rodents and bats, are small or only come out at night, so most people don't even realize they're there. But you can hardly miss a moose the size of a cow, or a hungry monkey that is pulling on your clothes for attention.

RING-TAILED COATI

A coati (say it "ko-wah-ti") will sniff out and eat more or less anything. The species travels in groups called bands, which scamper around with striped tails held high. In Central America, some people adore urban coatis and feed them, but others see them as pests.

Mammals are warm-blooded animals with fur or hair. Female mammals feed milk to their babies.

SLENDER LORIS

The Indian megacity Bangalore still has a few leafy parks with patches of forest. Here you can find the loris, a nighttime animal with giant goggly eyes that glow in the glare of a phone's flashlight. Beware: if you get too close, a loris's spit will give you a nasty rash.

LONG-TAILED MACAQUE

These urban monkeys can run riot. In the Malaysian capital Kuala Lumpur, they tug at people's clothing to beg for a snack. In Thailand, the mischievous macaques pull strands of hair from the heads of passersby. Human hair makes perfect dental floss!

JAPANESE SIKA DEER

In parts of Japan, it's completely normal to see deer walk past you on the sidewalk. These sika deer are said to be sacred, so people treat them with respect. Two places you can meet them are Miyajima (an island popular with tourists) and the temple city of Nara.

EUROPEAN HAMSTER

The main cemetery in Vienna, Austria, is hamster heaven. Hamsters might be the world's cheekiest animals—their super-stretchy cheek pouches can carry up to a fourth of their body weight in food. That's like an eight-year-old child stuffing their mouth with 4,000 strawberries.

MOOSE

"Watch out, there's a moose on the loose!" This is a real possibility in Anchorage, the biggest city in Alaska. It is surrounded by forests full of moose, which often wander into the city. Males, known as bulls, have huge antlers and a curious flap of wobbly skin under their chin.

RING-NECKED PARAKEET

With a shriek, some bright green birds flash past overhead. They are ring-necked parakeets, a type of long-tailed parrot. Originally from Africa and India, they are tough enough to survive cold winters in Europe.

Parakeets often visit bird feeders in Londoners' backyards.

Foxes are smaller than you might think – many pet cats are heavier!

Gray squirrels make curious chuffing sounds to attract a mate.

RED FOX

City foxes eat everything from earthworms to french fries dropped in the street. Nighttime is when they are the busiest, but by day you might spot them sunbathing on flat roofs or even strolling down the sidewalk. For some reason, they sometimes steal shoes and collect them in their dens.

RAT

There's an old saying that in London you are never more than 6 feet (1.8 m) from a rat. That's a slight exaggeration! Out of 100 buildings, probably only five will have a family of rats.

LONDON

In 2019, London became the world's first National Park City. This means the city is working to protect its green spaces, making it better for wildlife and healthier for people. Almost 9 million people live in the U.K. capital, but it's one of the best places in the country to see wild parakeets, foxes, and many other species.

A pair of **peregrine falcons** nests on the **Houses of Parliament.**

GRAY SEAL

The Thames River was heavily polluted in the past, but it's much cleaner now. Seals swim upstream from the Thames estuary to catch fish. Occasionally, one pops its head up for a breather in the middle of London.

EUROPEAN EEL

In the spring, a silver tide surges up the river. It is made up of thousands of baby eels, called elvers. These tiny fish have swum across the Atlantic Ocean to get here. They must continue past London, until they reach the upper sections of the Thames River, where they grow into adults.

Baby eels are **totally see-through,** like rice noodles.

CITY HERON

Herons build their messy nests in the trees in Battersea Park and Regent's Park, but they can be seen across the city, wherever there is water. They stand still as statues, waiting for a fishy meal to come near.

GOING UNDERGROUND

Beneath our feet lies a hidden world of wildlife. Under every city is a maze of basements, pipes, sewers, and drains. Many cities have subway trains—London's Tube network, for example, is 250 miles (400 km) long. These underground habitats are where you'll find insects, mice, rats, and bats. But you may also meet some more surprising creatures . . .

HOUSE MOUSE

One of these bright-eyed mammals can squeeze through a gap 0.4 inches (1 cm) wide. Forget what you see in cartoons—cheese is not their favorite food, but they do love sandwich crumbs. The London Underground is heaven for mice, because they have no predators and can look for snacks all day and night.

CELLAR SPIDER

In dark corners, you might spot these long-legged predators hanging from the roof. Though small, they have venom in their bite that's deadly to mosquitoes and other insects. If attacked, they flick sticky silk. Each spider's body has a marking like a human skull.

LONDON UNDERGROUND MOSQUITO

On the Tube it often reaches 77°F (25°C), and all that nice, warm air suits mosquitoes. These bloodsucking insects also have a plentiful supply of food down here—the passengers! The Tube mosquitoes are special, because they live only in tunnels—they're a different kind from the ones that bite us above ground.

ELEPHANT TRUNK SNAKE

After dark, one of the world's weirdest snakes comes out of hiding. Also called the Javan wart snake, it has loose, baggy skin that looks too big. It slithers into drains to hunt frogs.

RETICULATED PYTHON

During the rainy season, floodwater pours into the drains of this southern Asian megacity. Perfect for a python! This water-loving snake grows up to 20 feet (6 m) long. It can swim through the flooded pipes and tunnels to hunt rats. Special organs in its head detect the heat from its warm-blooded victims.

WATER MONITOR

Several hundred of these huge lizards stalk the parks of Bangkok. Big ones are as long as an adult human. They sneak into sewers, swimming to get around the crowded city. If you notice one lash its tail or hiss loudly, make your getaway: it's a warning.

Rascally **raccoons** are causing havoc in Berlin after being introduced from **North America**.

GOSHAWK

When this top forest predator is on the hunt, even other birds of prey need to be wary. Goshawks can target prey as large as woodpigeons and red squirrels. Many Berlin parks have goshawks nesting in them, including the Tiergarten, right next to parliament buildings in the middle of the city.

Berlin is home to **3,000–5,000 wild boar**, more than any other city in **Europe**.

WILD BOAR

Families of these wild pigs appear on the streets and in people's yards at sunset. The striped piglets might look cute to you, but not everyone appreciates wild boars. After they dig up flowerbeds and lawns to search for food, it looks like an excavator has run riot.

BERLIN

Germany is proud of its many nature-friendly cities. Its capital, Berlin, has some of Europe's most exciting wildlife, sometimes just feet away from passersby. More than a third of this busy city is either green (woods, parks, and gardens) or blue (canals and lakes).

NIGHTINGALE

A sweetly gorgeous song coming from a thick bush is probably a nightingale. Although the bird itself is brown and plain, its beautiful voice has long inspired authors and poets. Usually the nightingale lives in wetlands and woods, but it's common in Berlin.

In April and May, **nightingales** often sing at **night**, by the light of the moon.

HOODED CROW

All over the city you can see this gray-and-black bird, whose German name means "mist crow." It is naturally very curious and intelligent, and it can be taught to solve puzzles. In the winter, it has been spotted sliding down snow-covered roofs for fun!

HAWFINCH

That chunky beak delivers an enormous crushing force, the same as a 110-pound (50 kg) weight. Not bad for a small bird! The hawfinch uses it to split the pits of cherries, plums, and other fruit to reach the seeds inside.

SCAVENGERS

Drop bread or an apple core in the street and it won't last long—hungry wildlife will soon snap it up. Animals that eat food we throw away are called scavengers. They feast on all kinds of scraps, as well as on dead animals and plants. They can be as small as bugs or as big as bears. Without scavengers, our cities would end up knee-deep in waste.

POLAR BEAR

Seals are the favorite food of these mighty meat eaters. But sea ice in the Arctic is melting because of climate change, leaving the seals out of reach. Now starving, the bears wander into towns in northern Russia, Canada, and Alaska in search of a meal. Some have to be caught and relocated.

RACCOON

If you leave your door ajar in an American city, a raccoon might sneak inside your house to eat. Their nimble fingers can open refrigerators, lunch boxes, and garbage cans. Excellent climbers, they take over attics for their dens. In 2018, one raccoon climbed a 25-story building!

MARABOU STORK

As these giant birds soar through the skies of south and east Africa, they scan the ground below for dead animals such as zebras. Their huge beaks rip the bodies open. Messy garbage dumps outside cities attract these storks from far and wide, because our leftovers make an easy snack!

HERRING GULL

Watch out, gulls are about! Many British "seagulls" have swapped the coast for city living. They quickly learned that fast-food restaurants, public trash cans, and benches are where people carelessly drop food. Cities suit them for another reason too —nesting on flat roofs keeps their eggs and chicks safe from foxes.

SPOTTED HYENA

Hyenas are powerful hunters with bone-crunching jaws. At night in Ethiopia, some leave the grassy plains and slip into the old city of Harar. Here they visit street markets and garbage dumps to wolf down waste bones and pieces of meat. A few people even feed them by hand.

COCKROACH

Survivors from the time of the dinosaurs, these insects are super tough and can live almost anywhere on land. They'll eat virtually anything— even each other. Their antennae twitch constantly to pick up the smell of rotting food.

Huge **white-tailed eagles** sometimes visit the city in **winter.**

NUTHATCH

The nuthatch may remind you of a little woodpecker, but with one big difference. This is the only bird that climbs down trees headfirst instead of going up. Its feet are like tree anchors, with two strong claws pointing forward and two backward.

Everywhere you go in **Stockholm,** you will hear the cry of **gulls.**

STOCKHOLM

Stockholm is in northern Europe, beside the Baltic Sea. It is the capital of Sweden, and the environmental campaigner Greta Thunberg was born here. How fitting that Greta's home city is great for wildlife! In the parks, there are red squirrels, brown hares, and deer. There are even several families of beavers living on Stockholm's canals and waterways.

OSPREY

Stockholm's canals and coast are where you might see an osprey. An expert fisher, this bird of prey patrols slowly up and down, scanning the water below. With a sudden dive, it splashes down to catch a fish. Spines on the soles of its feet grip its slippery meal.

ROE DEER

A flash of white is often the first thing you notice as these small deer leap away and disappear into the trees. Their white backsides are a warning signal to each other. Roe deer can jump over fences and walls 6.5 feet (2 m) high, which helps them move around the city.

Roe deer are fond of nibbling flowers—gardeners, **watch out!**

OYSTERCATCHER

Strangely, oystercatchers don't eat that many oysters. Their favorite foods are mussels and clams, which they hammer or smash open to reach the juicy animal inside the shell. These shorebirds have a piping song, and pairs perform it as a duet, like black-and-white trumpeters.

EUROPEAN BEAVER

Wood and bark are food for these water-loving animals. They pile up sticks and branches to make a dam, which a pond forms behind. Their waterside home, built the same way, is called a lodge. Beavers benefit other wildlife because their hard work creates new habitats for fish, frogs, water beetles, and other species.

A **sudden splash** could be a **beaver**. They tail-slap the water when they sense **danger.**

33

A **screeching cry** means there's a jay in the area.

JAY

Leafy neighborhoods have oak trees, and wherever there are oak trees, you will find jays. These colorful crows love nothing better than acorns. In the fall, each bird can find and store 5,000 of them!

STONE MARTEN

An attic is a safe nesting place for a mother marten and her kits. When night falls, she emerges from the snug den to hunt birds, often snatching them off their perch as they sleep. She'll bring back rats and mice too. Male martens play no part in taking care of their young.

To mark their **territory**, martens pee on parked cars and **leave bite marks** in the engine wiring!

TREE SPARROW

In eastern Europe and Russia, these sparrows are a common sight in cities. You can tell them apart from house sparrows by the black spot on their cheek. Groups of them spend hours chattering away in bushes. They like weedy places, which in the summer are full of insects for their chicks.

WHITE STORK

Storks build their enormous stick nests on top of churches, chimneys, and city walls. In the spring, every pair keeps adding to their nest—some grow almost 10 feet (3 m) tall! Legends say that storks bring good luck, so people put up platforms to tempt them to stay and nest.

In old folk stories, **white storks** bring babies to families in their huge red bills.

BLACK REDSTART

What's that strange trill? It's a male black redstart, singing his heart out from a rooftop. The high-pitched song can carry a long way, over the din of traffic down below. "Start" is an old English word for tail, so you can see how the bird got its name.

From its lofty perch, a **black redstart** keeps an eye out for passing flies.

KRAKOW

The old town of Krakow, Poland, is hundreds of years old, with soaring towers and red-tiled roofs. This part of the beautiful city has not changed much since it was ruled by princes and kings. The ancient buildings are full of little nooks and quiet corners where wildlife can find a home.

MONK PARAKEET

Normally monk parakeets live in Argentina, but they were brought to Europe as pets. Now they're common in Seville and many other Spanish cities. You often catch sight of them in leafy streets and parks.

Male **cicadas** sing **all night long.**

The **Giralda**, or bell tower, is **340 feet (104 m) high**. That's the same as **34 school buses** on top of each other!

CICADA

When this bug stops moving, it matches the color of bark so well it almost disappears. On summer nights, it sings a high-pitched chirping song. Hundreds together sound like an insect orchestra.

SEVILLE

In the sunny south of Spain is Seville, the home of flamenco dancing. Some exciting and surprising animals have moved into its ancient buildings and tree-lined streets. As the sun sets, flocks of swifts zoom around the cathedral, and their screaming cries echo a great distance over the city.

MOORISH WALL GECKO

Crawling over walls are strange lizards. These are geckos, with giant googly eyes and the most amazing camouflage. They are on the lookout for insects to eat.

Speedy **swifts** look like **boomerangs** in the sky.

The favorite **prey** of lesser kestrels is **insects**, especially **grasshoppers**.

COMMON SWIFT

Hundreds of swifts nest on the cathedral. They can eat, drink, and even sleep as they fly. For the winter they migrate to Africa. Some of them fly nonstop for nine months!

LESSER KESTRAL

These rare kestrels live in big groups, or colonies, which is unusual for birds of prey. Look up and you will see many of their nests high up on the cathedral's stone ledges.

JACARANDA TREE

Every June, these trees burst into flower and turn Seville purple. Their sweet perfume might remind you of honey. Afterward, the fallen blossoms cover the city's parks and sidewalks.

Tangy **Seville oranges** are perfect for making **marmalade**. Yum!

AROUND THE HOME

Animals large and small have shared our homes since ancient times. Houses offer warmth and shelter as well as plenty to eat. Some of these visitors may be welcome—for example, house spiders catch flies and mosquitoes. Others are pests that eat our own food, chew through electrical wiring, or keep us awake at night. In some countries, a few animal guests can be dangerous if disturbed.

PEACOCK BUTTERFLY

Pretty European peacock butterflies flutter indoors to spend the winter in cool corners. Spare bedrooms and storage rooms are their favorite places. You might see one hibernating with its wings closed, clinging to a curtain. Touch it, and it will suddenly flick its wings open and hiss—a surprising trick that scares off most predators.

PIPISTRELLE BAT

In Old World houses, attics and lofts make a nursery for bats. A pipistrelle weighs about the same as three pennies put together, and it can fit in a matchbox, so crawling through gaps under the roof is no problem. In the summer, each female bat has a single tiny pup. At first, the bat baby is naked and sightless, but it grows fast on its mother's milk.

EDIBLE DORMOUSE

Scratch, scuffle, squeak . . . people soon know when one of these noisy mammals has moved in. Edible dormice make their summer nests in roof spaces across Europe. But they have a long hibernation, and spend up to eight months of every year asleep! Why the strange name? The Romans fattened these dormice up and ate them at feasts.

SILVERFISH

This is not a real fish, but a silvery, wriggly creature a little like a woodlouse or pill bug. Ancient insects similar to this began wriggling over Earth around 400 million years ago. Silverfish love nothing better than munching on flour, pasta, and oatmeal in kitchen cabinets.

FER-DE-LANCE

The fer-de-lance is one of the most venomous snakes in Central America. Near each of its eyes, there is a shallow pit. These are heat sensors that feel the warmth from the body of any animal nearby. Sometimes the snake follows a heat trail into sheds or houses to catch the rats it knows are there.

COMMON HOUSE GECKO

At night in Asian cities, this little lizard runs up and down walls and scoots across ceilings upside down. It can even climb the slippery glass in a window. What's its sticky secret? A gecko's feet have special sucker pads, covered with millions of microscopic hairs that give amazing grip. Their design has inspired new kinds of ultra-strong glue.

SYDNEY FUNNEL-WEB SPIDER

Most of the time, the funnel-web spider lives quietly in gardens in the Australian city of Sydney. It hides inside a silky burrow. But when the male spider goes in search of a mate, he may show up anywhere . . . and then people need to check their mailboxes and cars very carefully! Venom from his bite can kill a person in less than an hour.

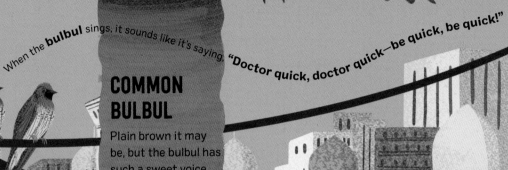

When the **bulbul** sings, it sounds like it's saying, "Doctor quick, doctor quick—be quick, be quick!"

COMMON BULBUL

Plain brown it may be, but the bulbul has such a sweet voice. In cities all over Africa, you can hear this bird's cheerful chatter coming from electricity wires and TV antennae.

Down by the river are **great egrets.** These elegant white **herons** hunt **fish** and **frogs.**

MEDITERRANEAN MANTIS

On a wall is a green insect with long legs, sitting so still it doesn't look alive. Meet the mantis—a fierce but patient predator whose giant eyes see in 3D, just like we do. No other insect has this superpower.

EGYPTIAN WEASEL

A weasel is a rat's worst nightmare. It can squeeze through rat-size gaps to chase its prey, and has jaws full of teeth as sharp as needles. Young weasels start eating meat when just three weeks old. By eight weeks, they can hunt on their own.

VIOLET CARPENTER BEE

What's making that loud buzz? She's bright purple and twice the size of a bumblebee—but don't worry, carpenter bees are harmless to you and me. This one has found the perfect place to raise her grubs—the hollow bamboo canes in a sunshade.

Weasels are the world's **smallest carnivores**—they're about as long as a pencil!

ALEXANDRIA

Two thousand years ago, Alexandria in Egypt was one of the most important cities in the ancient world. It faces the Mediterranean, near where the Nile River meets the sea, and it is still a busy port to this day. In the city's quieter corners you'll find birdsong and bees instead of traffic.

BARN SWALLOW

Ancient Egyptians were the first people to paint and carve swallows. These pretty birds are still a common sight in Egypt's cities today. They build their nests on buildings using many tiny beakfuls of mud. Each nest takes over a thousand trips to create.

HOUSE SPARROW

The sparrows pecking at crumbs under café tables are so tame one might even hop onto your shoe. The male with the biggest black chest is boss. He has the loudest chirp, owns the best nest on the street, and is most popular with the female sparrows.

Alexandria takes its name from **Alexander the Great,** the military ruler who created the city.

WILDLIFE HEROES

Animals living in cities face many threats. However, help is at hand. Cities are full of people who want to save the wildlife on their doorstep. These volunteers give up their evenings and weekends to rescue animals in danger. There are many other easy ways to be a wildlife hero, such as doing a survey. Even an hour of your time can make a difference.

TOAD RESCUE

On damp and drizzly evenings in the spring, common toads set off on a journey. They must reach a pond to lay their eggs. However, in cities, they have dangerous roads to cross. Luckily, local people set up toad patrols. The toad patrollers pick the toads up and carry them safely over.

WILDLIFE ART

Street artists, such as the London-based artist ATM, are covering walls with birds and beetles, tigers and trees. Their giant paintings show us the beauty of wildlife, and why we should protect the natural world. Owners of the buildings are also happy, because the colorful pictures brighten up the city. Passersby stop for a closer look, smile, and photograph the art.

BIG GARDEN BIRDWATCH

Each January, people in Great Britain take part in the Big Garden Birdwatch. The idea is simple. Everyone watches their bird feeders for an hour and keeps a list of which birds visit. They send in the results, and then a Top 20 of the most common birds is produced. The survey helps scientists see which birds are doing well and which need help.

CLEANUP CREW

One of the biggest dangers for African penguins is oil. Sometimes oil tankers spill their cargo at sea. When this happens, penguins end up covered in the thick, black goo. In this condition, their feathers are no longer waterproof. Without help, they would soon die. Volunteers in Cape Town, South Africa, rescue the oiled penguins and clean them up.

BIRD HOSPITAL

Two brothers in the Indian city of Delhi have set up a bird hospital. Nadeem and Mohammed's backyard is full of cages and equipment. Most of the patients are birds of prey called black kites, which live all over the city. Often the kites arrive with cuts or broken wings. The brothers take care of them until they heal and can be set free.

TURTLE SOS

Baby turtles are just 4 inches (10 cm) long and weigh the same as 6 sheets of paper. They hatch at night from nests on beaches, then wiggle down to the sea. But the lights of hotels and bars in seaside cities can dazzle them. The confused hatchlings go the wrong way and walk up the beach by mistake. In Australia, teams are on standby to save the tiny turtles before crabs or birds eat them.

CHACMA BABOON

These adaptable animals get into all kinds of trouble in Cape Town. They steal food from café tables, climb over vehicles, and raid people's kitchens. Today over 500 of them live in the city, which some people think is too many. There are fines for feeding baboons, as it encourages them to monkey around.

CAPE WHITE-EYE

A pretty little bird perched in a bush or tree is probably this one. It hardly ever stays still, and flits to and fro in search of its next meal. Flower nectar and insects are its favorite foods.

Cape Town is the **second-biggest city** in **South Africa**, and probably the most **beautiful.**

AGAPANTHUS

Scientists refer to this part of Africa as the Cape Floral Kingdom. That's because it has so many amazing plants that don't grow anywhere else in the wild. One is a tall blue flower called agapanthus, or the African lily. You can see it all over Cape Town.

CAPE TOWN

Cape Town is at the very tip of Africa, as far south as you can go. It's the only place with both penguins and monkeys. Table Mountain towers over the city, and the cold Atlantic Ocean meets the warm Indian Ocean. Strong currents bring food for great schools of fish, which in turn are food for lots of other sea life.

AFRICAN PENGUIN

Look—a penguin parade! You often see penguins walking around Simon's Town, a suburb not far from Cape Town. Up to 3,000 of them nest on its quiet beach. There are fewer African penguins than there used to be, so this urban colony is protected. Viewing platforms let people watch the penguins safely.

Great white sharks cruise up and down the coast in the summer.

African penguins live on small, silvery fish called sardines.

BLACK GIRDLED LIZARD

Look out for this lizard sunning itself on a rock. Local people call it the "sun seeker," because it turns to face the sun (which is dangerous for us). The lizard's spiky scales are tough armor and make it look a bit like a small crocodile.

ANIMALS ON THE MOVE

Much of the wildlife in cities is just visiting. Animals come and go, like tourists or people on their way to and from work. Some might explore a city during the day, or travel around it after dark. Others stay there to raise a family. Animals on long journeys sometimes use cities like we use travel plazas, as somewhere to eat and rest.

BROAD-WINGED HAWK

Many birds make long flights called migrations, on which they often pass cities. Birds that go between North and South America fly over Panama City, where they fill the sky. Among the great flocks are many broad-winged hawks. The city's skyscrapers are useful landmarks that they recognize from their last journey.

SEA TROUT

Stockholm, Sweden, is a watery city, with many rivers and canals. Sea trout swim into them in the fall, after growing fat and strong at sea. They travel upstream to where they first hatched. Every fish remembers the taste and smell of its own river, which helps it find the way home. When they arrive, the female trout lay their eggs.

FALLOW DEER

When London is asleep, a herd of deer come out to explore. By day, they stay near the city in Epping Forest. Their white spots hide them among the trees. By night, the deer walk along the quiet streets and empty sidewalks. They look for fresh grass and even visit people's yards.

MEXICAN FREE-TAILED BAT

In the summer a million bats live under a single American bridge. A million! The bats tuck into small gaps in Congress Avenue Bridge in Austin, Texas. At sunset, they rush out into the sky, and crowds of people watch them go. All night long the bats hunt insects in the countryside, then before dawn they fly back to the city.

BOGONG MOTH

These Australian moths look ordinary, but they do something amazing. They can cover entire buildings like a giant brown blanket. Inside a swarm, there may be thousands of moths per square yard. The mega swarms happen when the moths are flying past cities in the night sky. Bright lights attract them, and they land in a storm of wings.

DOG-FACED FRUITBAT

Singapore's bridges give these bats a safe place to sleep. At night the bats visit trees to eat fruit, and after their meal they scatter the fruit seeds in their poop. In this way, they help new trees grow—they are very important to the city's forests.

Giant **supertrees** made of concrete and steel tower over the bay. **Real plants** grow on their trunks.

WHITE-THROATED KINGFISHER

This gorgeous bird sits by the water's edge until it sees a movement. Then, as quick as a flash, it dives to catch its prize. As well as fish, the kingfisher eats crabs and insects.

Sunbirds hang their nests from **twigs** to keep their **chicks safe** from **snakes.**

OLIVE-BACKED SUNBIRD

If you watch flowers in the city's parks, it won't be long before you see sunbirds. Using their curved beaks, they reach inside the blooms to sip the sweet nectar. In the sunshine, their plumage glitters like precious gems.

Local people share updates of the **latest otter sightings** on social media.

PAINTED JEZEBEL

Butterflies are a common sight throughout the city. The jezebel has bright colors, which are a warning to birds. They are like a message saying, "I taste bad!" so that the butterfly is left alone.

SINGAPORE

This island megacity is in southern Asia, just north of the equator. Not long ago, it was a fishing village, with rain forest and swamps all around it. In just 200 years, it has grown into one of the busiest ports on the planet. Downtown Singapore has many shiny new buildings, but it's also a very green city, full of wildlife.

Singapore means **"Lion City."** Big cats did once roam the forest here—but they were tigers, not lions.

One-third of Singapore is covered with trees. The city plants more than **50,000 new trees** a year.

LOTUS FLOWER
Ponds in Singapore are often covered with white and pink lotus flowers. The lotus is sacred to many Hindus and Buddhists. They believe the flower is a sign of beauty, honesty, and good health. It is also a symbol of the Sun.

SMOOTH-COATED OTTER
A family of otters lives in Marina Bay, in the heart of the city. Their smooth bodies and powerful paws make them superb swimmers. People often see the otters fishing in the water or playing together on the shore. After a swim, they spend a long time grooming, to keep their fur waterproof.

WHITE-BREASTED WATERHEN
Waterhens creep across the lotus leaves that float on the water. These birds have very long legs and toes, so they can walk over the leaves without falling in. They croak like frogs and bob their heads backward and forward like chickens.

MUMBAI

Mumbai, India, is home to more than 20 million people, making this megacity one of the biggest in the world. It's a busy, bustling place. But at night, Mumbai shows a wilder side. Snakes, big cats, and many other creatures appear from their daytime hiding places.

People keep pet **mongooses** to kill **rats** and **mice**.

SPOTTED DEER

Herds of deer live in patches of woods around the city. Grass is their normal food, but they don't mind nibbling bags of garbage too, which is pretty unusual for deer!

Civets spray a **strong smell** to mark their **home patch.**

PALM CIVET

These slinky animals look like they are half-cat and half-weasel, but one of their Indian names is "tree dog." Their squealing and scampering can keep people awake.

INDIAN COBRA

After dark, cobras slither around backyards and sheds to catch their favorite prey—rats and other snakes. If people frighten them and they bite someone, their venom may be deadly.

INDIAN GRAY MONGOOSE

A mongoose may have a face like a stuffed animal, but it's one of the few creatures able to fight and kill big snakes, even cobras. It has to be quick!

HANUMAN LANGUR

In a jungle, langurs sleep high up trees to be safe from leopards. In the city, they are just as happy to use empty buildings or electricity poles.

LEOPARD

Many leopards prowl Sanjay Gandhi National Park, which is part of Mumbai. At night, they are bold enough to come onto the city's streets to hunt stray dogs and wild pigs.

In 2018, researchers counted **47 adult leopards** and **eight cubs** in the national park.

Langurs like to **monkey around** on balconies and roofs.

CITIES AT NIGHT

Our cities are still full of life when the Sun goes down. As daytime creatures settle down for the night, many others wake up. Animals that come out at night are called nocturnal animals. As well as bats, there are species such as foxes, badgers, and weasels. The night shift also includes some amazing insects and birds.

EURASIAN BADGER

Eurasian badgers are carnivores (animals with meat-eating teeth). But they're not picky, and they feast on everything from worms to berries. Most badgers live in woods and fields. But there are some in Bristol, Brighton, and several other English cities, usually in quiet places such as graveyards. Each family of about six badgers spends the day in a burrow, called a sett. Only when it's dark do their striped faces appear.

EAGLE OWL

These are the world's largest owls, with a wingspan longer than your bed. Their usual habitat is mountains and forests, where they nest on cliffs. Recently, the birds have moved into cities in Germany, Austria, and Finland, nesting on buildings instead. Rabbits, foxes, squirrels, and rats all need to look out when these huge owls are around.

SIBERIAN WEASEL

In old parts of the Chinese capital Beijing, people often hear strange noises on their roof at night. Pitter-patter, pitter-patter, what could it be? It's probably one of the local weasels. These little hunters are like acrobats as they run around the backstreets in search of mice. Their nickname in China is "yellow rat wolves."

CECROPIA MOTH

At night this huge moth flutters into gardens and backyards. It's the largest moth in North America. The spots on its wings look like big eyes staring at you, which gives birds a shock. The tricked birds go and find a less scary meal, and the moth escapes. Like many moths, it doesn't eat, and it dies after just a few weeks.

NANKEEN NIGHT HERON

Nankeen is an old word meaning "yellowish," which is how these handsome herons got their name. They rest in trees in the daytime, and at night go fishing. In Australian cities such as Melbourne, the herons like to visit backyard ponds. The next morning, people might find they have a few goldfish missing.

FIREFLY

No, this is not actually a fly, but a beetle. How confusing! Its other name is "lightning bug," which gives a clue to what its special skill is. In the dark it glows yellow and is able to flash on and off. This is a signal that the female firefly uses to get the attention of a male firefly. You can see the dazzling light show in New York's Central Park.

WINTER JASMINE

When the winter snow melts, this bush bursts into bloom. In China it is known as "the flower that welcomes spring." Its cheerful yellow petals form little stars and put people in a good mood.

Winters in Beijing are **very cold,** with lots of snow and ice, but **summers** are **long and hot.**

ASIAN SWALLOWTAIL

A pair of long "tails" give this beautiful butterfly its name. But its caterpillars look just like moist, spongy bird droppings. What an excellent disguise! Hungry birds are tricked, because they don't want to put their beak in poop. So the caterpillars are safe, and the birds stay hungry.

Emperor Yongle created this park **600 years ago**, as a gift to keep the gods happy.

BEIJING

Few cities are as ancient as China's capital, Beijing. It is enormous—ten times larger than London and still growing. But wildlife can find refuge in the parks here. One of the most famous parks is at the Temple of Heaven. This oasis of calm used to be just for the ruling emperor. Today, it's open to everyone.

HOOPOE

This is a bird that sings its own name: hoo-poe, hoo-poe, hoo-poe. If it is excited, it spreads the black-and-white feathers on top of its head to make a fan. As it takes off, it looks like a giant butterfly.

MAGNOLIA TREE

Magnolia trees have spectacular blossoms. The large flowers are pink or white and smell like vanilla. Later, the trees produce strange-looking fruits that are red and knobbly.

AZURE-WINGED MAGPIE

Most parks in Beijing are home to these magpies. Usually they go around in flocks, hopping through the trees together. Chinese people call them the "happy bird." Should you hear one sing, it is supposed to bring good luck.

SIBERIAN CHIPMUNK

These small squirrels run around the park's rock garden. At times they can be quite friendly, and take food when people offer it. The mothers have two litters a year, one in the spring and another in the summer.

MANDARIN DUCK

The male Mandarin is fabulously colorful. He even has a pair of orange "sails," which are actually curved feathers. The female Mandarin nests in a tree hole. When her ducklings hatch, they can't fly and have to jump all the way down to the ground.

Chipmunks have an **excellent memory.** They need it to find all the **seeds** they hide!

BUGS AND BEES

It's amazing how many insects and other creepy-crawlies live in our cities. Scientists call them "invertebrates," which means they have no backbone. Though small, these creatures do lots of useful things. They pollinate flowers, help us produce food, and carry our garbage away. So next time you see an ant in the street, or a beetle in the park, leave it alone. It has an important job to do!

PEPPERED MOTH

In the 1800s, English scientists noticed something odd about these moths. Some were white, but others were almost totally black. In cities, most of the moths were dark ones. Being dark hid them against tree trunks, which were dirty because of sooty black smoke from chimneys. Tree trunks are paler now that cities are cleaner, so today white moths are more common again.

STAG BEETLE

A beetle battle is taking place on a log. Two male stag beetles are trying to push each other off, in a test of strength. Their huge jaws look like the antlers of a stag (male deer). Stag beetles are found in London parks, but most of their life is spent underground as fat white grubs, munching dead wood, before they turn into adult beetles.

BLACK GARDEN ANT

These ants nest under sidewalks and patios. On a hot summer's day, they come out through the cracks in great black swarms. The ants have wings, and soon take flight. Among them are a few queen ants. Each queen will head off to start a new ant colony.

Billions of black garden ants **take to the sky** on the same day. No one knows how they get the **timing right**.

HONEYBEE

Honeybees find plenty of nectar in cities. They fly up to 2 miles (3 km) away to visit the flowers in parks and gardens, beside roads, and even on balconies. In the middle of Paris, beekeepers keep rooftop hives. Each hive may have 50,000 female worker bees. Because these bees all hatched from eggs laid by the hive's queen bee, they are all sisters!

SCARCE SWALLOWTAIL

This tiger-striped beauty is one of the most stunning butterflies in Europe. You see it in southern cities such as Athens, the capital of Greece. When the swallowtail flies, it is so elegant it seems to float through the air. Its caterpillars feed on the leaves of cherry and almond trees.

PORTUGUESE MILLIPEDE

The name millipede means "a thousand feet." In fact, these animals normally only have 50–100 pairs, but that's still a lot of legs. Millipedes are ancient creatures, even older than the dinosaurs. Swarms of them may suddenly appear in cities in Australia, China, and Japan. They taste foul, so anything that picks them up gets a nasty shock.

57

歌舞伎

TOKYO

Tokyo, Japan, is the biggest city the world has ever seen. It's actually four cities joined together. Part of this vast urban area is built on new land created from the sea. To survive in such a crowded place, animals have had to change their behavior. They have learned how to get around the busy streets, and have figured out some clever ways of finding food.

In **2019**, the Tokyo area was home to **37 million people.**

CARRION CROW

In Japan's cities, crows have a neat way of cracking nuts. They perch on a traffic light, drop a nut onto the street, then wait for vehicles to drive over it. When the light turns red and the traffic stops, they fly down to collect the smashed nut.

好きて

とごし

焼烏釜めし

戸越

マッサージ

華宴

すし雰蒲焼

カキ
フライ

RACCOON DOG

These super-furry animals look a bit like raccoons, and a bit like dogs. Their coats are thick to protect from cold winters. Japanese people call them tanuki. According to legends, they can change shape and become humans!

Raccoon dogs use **gutters and drains** to **explore** the city.

Raccoon dogs will **eat** just about anything. They often use **gutters and drains** to **explore** the city.

VARIED TIT

Tokyo's temple gardens and lines of street trees are like tiny patches of forest. They provide a leafy habitat for small birds such as this one. Often you hear its cheerful song before you spot the bird itself.

When Japan's cherry trees come into **blossom** in the spring, there is a **national festival.** Millions of people enjoy the **party.**

ORIENTAL TURTLE DOVE

This dove has beautiful pink-and-brown feathers. You can see it perched in street trees, such as Tokyo's many cherry trees. It has a soft call that sounds like purring.

JAPANESE TOAD

Swamps and forests are the usual home of these toads, but they also live in some city parks. In the spring, they have to travel to ponds to breed. As they walk there, they pop up in flowerbeds, on sidewalks, and in other strange places.

Small **earthquakes** are common in this city. All buildings have to be **quake-proof.**

JAPANESE RHINOCEROS BEETLE

With its massive horn, this beetle is a popular pet in Japan. However, it often escapes and flies away from its owner. Escaped beetles can be seen as they wander around the city. The male rhino beetles use their horns in fights—they try to flip each other into the air.

LAUGHING KOOKABURRA

The kookaburra is a kingfisher bigger than a pigeon. It likes to perch on a post or wire for a better view. From up here, it swoops to catch small lizards and snakes. Sometimes it grabs meat off barbecue grills! Its loud cry sounds like a laugh.

GRAY-HEADED FLYING FOX

During the day, these big bats sleep upside down in groups. We call them flying foxes because of their furry bodies and fox-like faces. They eat fruit and can fly 30 miles (50 km) a night to find fresh supplies.

Sail out of **Sydney Harbor** and you will meet the wide-open **Pacific Ocean.**

*Gum trees are the main type of tree in Australia. They have **flaky bark** and **spectacular flowers.***

RAINBOW LORIKEET

Many Australian cities have these rainbow-colored parrots. Flocks of them visit gum trees to feed from the red and pink flowers. The birds lap up the sugary flower nectar greedily. To make the job easier, the tip of their tongue is shaped like a mop.

SYDNEY

Thousands of years ago, there was a beautiful river valley in Australia. Then the sea level rose, and the ocean flooded the valley to create a huge bay. Its sparkling waters are now called Sydney Harbor, and the largest city in Australia has grown up around it. On one shore is the Royal Botanic Garden, full of plants from all over the country.

COMMON BRUSH-TAIL POSSUM

Wherever there are trees in Sydney, you're bound to find brush-tail possums. They love life in the Botanic Garden, which has many different leaves, flowers, and fruit for them to feed on. Excellent climbers, the possums nest inside hollow trees and under roofs.

The white roofs of the **Sydney Opera House** are based on the segments of an orange.

Like kangaroos, mother possums keep their babies in a pouch on their belly.

EASTERN WATER DRAGON

Hot, dry Australia is heaven for reptiles. Hundreds of different lizard and snake species live there. This lovely lizard is common in Sydney, and is an expert insect hunter. It also likes water and may swim in search of food.

EASTERN BROWN SNAKE

This snake spends a lot of time hiding among dry leaves. Being brown is great camouflage. Stepping on it is very bad news, because it has powerful venom. It hunts mice in quiet corners of the Botanic Garden.

61

MAKING WILDLIFE WELCOME

Cities are often great for wildlife, but we can make them even better. A good place to start is in our backyards. We can leave wild corners, add a pond, put up nest boxes for birds, and stop using chemicals to kill bugs. We can also make simple changes to our buildings and streets to make them more wildlife-friendly.

HEDGEHOG HIGHWAYS

Old World hedgehogs walk 1 mile (1.5 km) every night to sniff out worms, beetles, slugs, and caterpillars for their supper. They love living in backyards, but there's a problem. Fences and walls keep them from getting around and finding enough food. If a person makes a 5 x 5 inch (13 x 13 cm) hole in the bottom of their fence, the hogs can squeeze through and move from one yard to the next.

WILDLIFE PONDS

A small pond is one of the best things you can add to a yard. Within 24 hours, the first insects arrive. Often these are dragonflies, or water striders that slide across the surface of the water. Ponds also give a home to frogs and water snails. Birds come to bathe, and thirsty animals such as foxes visit to drink. Even a tiny pond is a valuable habitat for wildlife.

GREEN ROOFS

Roofs can be turned into meadows that buzz with life. These are sometimes called "green roofs." One example is in Copenhagen, the capital of Denmark. Here the roof of an indoor ski slope has been covered with soil and planted with flowers and trees. This meadow in the sky is visited by bumblebees and butterflies.

LIGHTS OUT

Skyscrapers that light up the night are a danger to birds. When birds fly over cities, the glow down below can attract them. Sadly, many die as they crash into the buildings. Cities such as Chicago now turn off the lights in their tallest towers to stop birds from flying too close.

MONKEY SANCTUARIES

In India, there is a tradition that monkeys are holy animals. Many temples have statues and carvings of the Hindu monkey god. Real monkeys, called macaques, also live in the temples. They know they are safe here, because people protect them. Visitors bring food and drink for the macaques, which have become tame.

NEST TOWERS

Purple martins nest in backyards in the middle of American cities. Long ago, these birds nested in trees. None do that today. They prefer to use the special wooden boxes that people put up. The boxes provide a safe place for the martins to lay eggs and rear their chicks.

PLANTING TREES

Trees in cities are more than just decoration. They give us shade, clean the air, and help fight climate change. Trees also make us feel better! Scientists find that we are healthier if we live in streets lined with trees. In Chinese cities, there are huge projects to plant thousands more trees. The greenery will reduce the pollution from vehicles and factories.

INDEX